Free TO Worship
Liberated TO Praise

A Biblical Guide To Worship

Pastor Elenora Mouphouet

Published by

DAYELight
PUBLISHERS

ISBN: 978-1-953759-58-0 (paperback)

Scripture quotations marked "KJV" are taken from the Holy Bible, King James Version (Public Domain).

Scripture quotations marked "NKJV" are taken from the New King James Version. Copyright © 1982 by Thomas Nelson, Inc. Used by permission. All rights reserved. Bible text from the New King James Version® is not to be reproduced in copies or otherwise by any means except as permitted in writing by Thomas Nelson, Inc., Attn: Bible Rights and Permissions, P.O. Box 141000, Nashville, TN 37214-1000.

Scripture quotations marked (NIV) are taken from the Holy Bible, New International Version®, NIV®. Copyright © 1973, 1978, 1984 by Biblica, Inc.™ Used by permission of Zondervan. All rights reserved worldwide.

Dedication

To my heavenly Father, who called me to the ministry when I did not think I was worth it. Words cannot express my gratitude. I will serve You with every second of my life, with You being by my side.

To my love, my husband, Apostle Edward Mouphouet, you have been my constant support, my mentor, and most of all, an excellent example of what it means to be sold out for the gospel of Jesus Christ. I love sharing life moments with you, and to Mr. Genius (DEM), you came along and made our lives joyful; thanks for being you.

To my parents, I will forever be grateful to you for aligning with God's purpose for my life by deciding not to abort me; thanks for being the best mom.

Acknowledgment

The completion of this book would not have been possible without the participation and assistance of many people; their contributions are highly appreciated and gratefully acknowledged.

In truth, I could not have completed this book without a strong support team.

Thanks to my heavenly Father, who woke me at odd hours to write this book.

Thanks to my team of "critique readers," who read my book and gave me their honest opinions and advice.

Thanks to my hubby for his direction and mentoring. Thanks for your unwavering support.

I want to express my gratitude to my editors, Sara Watts of Sara Editing, and DayeLight Publishing.

Table of Content

Dedication.. iii

Acknowledgment... v

Preface 9

Chapter One: A HEART FILLED WITH GRATITUDE 11

Chapter Two: WORSHIP DEFINED 15

Chapter Three: THE MINISTRY OF PRAISE AND WORSHIP. 25

Chapter Four: DIFFERENT KINDS OF WORSHIP 37

Chapter Five: PRAISE 41

Chapter Six: HEBREW WORDS FOR PRAISE 51

Chapter Seven: THE BENEFITS OF PRAISE AND WORSHIP.. 61

Chapter Eight: PRAISE AND WORSHIP EXPRESSIONS 71

Chapter Nine: RESOURCES 85

Conclusion... 91

Bibliography 93

Author's Bio 95

Preface

Writing this book comes from my passion to see the principles of true worship restored in the body of Christ. As our presentation of worship shifts over the years, one thing remains and will always remain: *But the hour cometh, and now is, when the true worshippers shall worship the Father in spirit and in truth: for the Father seeketh such to worship him. God is a Spirit: and they that worship him must worship him in spirit and in truth. (John 4:23-24 – KJV).* My earnest prayer is that you glean from this book and join the radical few who are true worshipers.

Chapter One

A HEART FILLED WITH GRATITUDE

In everything give thanks; for this is the will of God in Christ Jesus for you. (1 Thessalonians 5:18 – NKJV).

Oh, give thanks to the Lord, for He is good! For His mercy endures forever. (Psalm 107:1 – NKJV).

Thanks, or gratitude, plays a vital role in how we express praise and worship. Appreciation adds emotion and enthusiasm to our worship. When we recognize all the things our Father does for us, our worship flows from the deepest place of our hearts. One may say, I have not received any miracle or seen any change in my circumstance, so my worship is on a plateau. However, the fact that He saved us from the grips of hell and the plans of the enemy should shake us to the very core of our being, giving us an endless attitude of gratitude. It is in the Word of God that we find our spiritual identity and discover our purpose. Salvation is another reason why gratitude should flow from our hearts like a stream that never runs dry.

Gratefulness is a conscious effort to show appreciation for what has been done for you, even when it seems like nothing. Gratitude should be directed to the Giver of the gift, and not the gift received. Most of the time, we are not grateful because we measure our appreciation based on what we believe we should have. We bring the same attitude to the body of Christ when we receive Jesus Christ as our Lord, thereby making it difficult to participate in worship. If we can change our mindset, our worship can be efficacious.

Enhancing Your Understanding Of Praise And Worship

The Hebrew and Greek languages are rich in context and offer a broad perspective for the study of the Bible; every word in each of these languages is nuanced—they could have more than one definition, and when translated, the appropriate word that fits the sentence is used. It is essential to know the original meaning of the words used to describe praise and worship for a better understanding and in-depth study. These were the exact words used by the spiritual forefathers to worship the Lord. Understanding the meaning of these words from the Hebrew and Greek perspective will enrich our understanding. Understanding will give you confidence and strengthen your worship. As worship leaders, we neglect this aspect of our worship. The English language is limited in translation, but the Hebrew and Greek languages provide different words that express one thing.

Instruments As A Driving Force

Without some form of musical instruments, worship songs and worship leading would be incomplete. Of course, musical instruments do not minimize the power of the beautiful sounds of Acapella and making beautiful melodies with our voices. Still, we can all agree that instrumentations can take beautiful lyrics to another level of worship. Music, without dispute, is a powerful tool that appeals to humanity, and if added to God-given songs, it can work wonders in the heart of men. Our Father, God, is a creator of music, and He has gifted people as the psalmists in the Bible that used their instruments to worship God, cast out tormenting spirits, and call down the glory of God, and it can be an excellent tool in the hand of the worship leader. When we learn to combine the two, we can touch the hearts of many.

> All the Levites who were musicians—Asaph, Heman, Jeduthun and their sons and relatives—stood on the east side of the altar, dressed in fine linen and playing cymbals, harps and lyres. They were accompanied by 120 priests sounding trumpets. The trumpeters and musicians joined in unison to give praise and thanks to the Lord. Accompanied by trumpets, cymbals and other instruments, the singers raised their voices in praise to the Lord and sang "He is good; His love endures forever." Then the temple of the Lord was filled with the cloud, and the priests could not perform their service because of the cloud, for the glory of the Lord filled the temple of God. (2 Chronicles 5:12-14 – NIV).

It was a joint effort on this glorious day. The Levites sang, and the musicians or instrumentalists played beautiful melodies. As they played, God was pleased with their worship, and He responded with a glorious visitation. Instruments blended with melodious voices can move the hand of God, and God is pleased when we play skillfully.

13

> Now the Spirit of the Lord had departed from Saul, and an evil spirit from the Lord tormented him. Whenever the spirit from God came on Saul, David would take up his lyre and play. Then relief would come to Saul; he would feel better, and the evil spirit would leave him (1 Samuel 16:14, 23 – NIV).

David played the harp, and Saul received deliverance from demonic oppression. In this passage of scripture, we see a different effect of music. David was not in a temple, neither was he in a band, but the result is still profound. He played, and the presence of God descended to provide deliverance for King Saul.

In closing, the instruments did not provoke heaven, but the Levites who played, so as we strive to play instruments to glorify God, let us not forget that we must live a consecrated life.

Chapter Two

WORSHIP DEFINED

Old Testament

Worship is an expression of strong devotion; it is an outburst of genuine love and holy reverence for a holy God. Therefore, by following the principles in Romans 10, we believe that Jesus Christ of Nazareth is Lord and we ask Him to become our Lord and Savior:

> That if you confess with your mouth the Lord Jesus and believe in your heart that God has raised Him from the dead, you will be saved. For with the heart one believes unto righteousness, and with the mouth confession is made unto salvation (Romans 10:9-10 – NKJV).

We believe in our hearts and confess with our mouths that Jesus is Lord by accepting Him. Jesus becomes our Master and Saviour. Once that decision is made, we have signed up to begin a journey of worship to none other than our first love, the Creator of heaven and earth, Abba Father-God. *"Then saith Jesus unto him, get thee hence, Satan: for it is written, Thou shalt worship the Lord thy God,*

15

and him only shalt thou serve…" (Matthew 4:10 – KJV). We are to have no other gods besides our GOD, our Father, the Creator of the heavens and the earth. We are to worship no other gods besides our Father, as it is written, *"Thou shalt have no other gods before me" (Exodus 20:3 – KJV)*. Nothing and no one can take the place of our Father. He alone is to be worshipped as our God and Master. All others are to be placed second in our lives, including spouses, children, jobs, and money; it may sound harsh, but it is the truth. When we accept Jesus into our lives, we begin to learn how to be good stewards of our lives and everything we have, including realigning our priorities, and that includes worship as well.

The Bible gives a clear illustration as to how worship should look in the scripture listed below:

> Oh come, let us worship and bow down; Let us kneel before the Lord our Maker! (Psalm 95:6 – NKJV).

True worship is the kind of worship our Father deserves: worship that flows from a heart of reverence and humility. The Hebrew word for worship in these scriptures is **"Shachah"** (the Touch Bible) which means to bow down, to depress, to prostrate oneself before a superior in homage, for example, before God in Worship or to royalty: to bow (self) down, crouch, fall down (flat), humbly beseech, do (make) obeisance, do reverence, make to stoop, worship. Then he said, "Lord, I believe!" And he worshiped Him (See John 9:38). In Greek, the word is **"Proskuneo,"** meaning "to kiss the hand towards one, in token of reference, like a dog licking the hand of his master, to fawn or crouch to, homage (do reverence to, adore), to make obedience, prostrate oneself in homage, to fall upon the knees and to touch the ground with the forehead as an expression of profound reference: to worship."

New Testament

There are a few words in the New Testament that describe or defines worship:

Sebomai: "to revere, to worship, to adore and to offer religious worship, to offer devotion to God."

> Saying, this fellow persuadeth men to worship God contrary to the law. (Acts 18:13 – KJV).

Latreuo: "To minister to, to serve, to render religious service or homage, to perform sacred service, to worship, to worship God in the observance of the rites instituted for His worship (according to biblical standards)."

> For we are the circumcision, which worships God in the spirit, and rejoice in Christ Jesus, and have no confidence in the flesh. (Philippians 3:3 – KJV).

Believers cannot worship according to man's wisdom or man's understanding. Therefore, we must honor the Father in worship according to His Word and principles.

Worship in this present age has become a way of showing off talents by singing songs and making a joyful noise. However, worship extends far beyond lyrics, rhythm, verses, bridge of a song and far above the worship ministry of a church or a worship band. In our services, it goes beyond praise and worship time. When we sing, we express who our God is to us, but it is a testament to the world and a proclamation of our reverence to Him when we live out our worship to Him. Hence, worship is a lifestyle that all believers must cultivate.

> I beseech you therefore, brethren, by the mercies of God, that you present your bodies a living sacrifice, holy, acceptable to God, which is your reasonable service. (Romans 12:1 – NKJV).

True worship goes far beyond our feelings and thinking. It should affect our lives and influence our daily lives. Therefore, we must willingly embrace true worship according to the Word of God, even if it will cost us.

A Command

> But the hour is coming, and now is, when the true worshipers will worship the Father in spirit and truth; for the Father is seeking such to worship Him. God is Spirit, and those who worship Him must worship in spirit and truth. (John 4:23-24 – NKJV).

In this passage, God seeks and is expecting to find sold-out worshippers, Spirit-led believers who will humble themselves in worship; will you answer the call?

To command means to give an authoritative order. A command can only be given by a person with authority. Every citizen of the United States of America and all its inhabitants ought to obey the laws of the land. Our disagreement or dislike of a law does not give us the right to break the law. When you represent a kingdom, you live by the rules of the kingdom you represent. As believers and children of God, we have been commanded to worship our Father in spirit and in truth.

There is no way you can be a child of God and choose which commandment to follow or obey. We must obey the totality of the Word of God; we cannot pick and choose based on how we feel or what we think it should be—that includes the way we express ourselves in worship. We must seek knowledge about a given command and make a conscious effort to follow what the word of God stipulates. Sometimes, the Word of God challenges our belief system, our former way of life, or thought pattern; however, we must have no excuse. A command must be obeyed, followed, and carried out without hesitation.

The lifestyle of worship is a command. Every child of God should be willing to live and pursue a daily life that expresses worship to our King. It is when worship becomes a lifestyle that a believer can genuinely express worship. It is a heart thing, which comes by building up a personal relationship with our Father. When we get to know Him, it becomes easier to talk to Him, describe Him, and bow before Him in true worship. Most of the time allotted to express our worship carries a tone of a resounding gong, missing the power and communion of the Holy Spirit because we do not know our Father, and therefore, we cannot relate to Him. Just as it is impossible to fellowship with or love a stranger, it will be impossible to express worship to our Father simply because we do not know Him personally. If we want to see a move of God in our services, communities, and the world and have God take His seat amidst His people and have encounters with the Spirit of God, we must spend time with Him. When we follow biblical principles of worship, it is easy to express worship daily.

We all strive to obey the Word of God in other areas of our lives. Following God's Word on worship and how to worship is also vital to our Christian walk. It is impossible to serve the Lord in other areas of our lives and disobey His command on how He wants to receive worship from us. Worship leaders are simply the vessels God uses to lead His people to the throne of grace, at the feet of Jesus, but these are the people God placed in authority in that area. Keep in mind, that when a worship leader asks you to worship, it is not because they want to command you, but rather that they understand worship and know how to guide you in worship. View the instructions from the Father through the person currently in use.

We may not think of these things as disobedience, but they are. If the scripture is clear about something, and a child of God refuses to abide by the Word of God, then they fall into sin because the Bible lets us know:

> Therefore, to him who knows to do good and does not do it, to him it is sin. (James 4:17 – NKJV).

Sometimes, we pick and choose how we want to obey the scriptures. We must be careful how we offer worship or how we neglect worship, lest we fall short of the grace of God. We go to a church and are concerned about what people will think or say about us when we look undignified during worship—the body of Christ has become more man-conscious than God-conscious. When a commanding officer of an army gives an order, his subordinates do not question him; they perform the assignment. Likewise, believers must obey God's Word concerning worship.

Personal Or Private Worship

The Bible is not shy about words on the expression of worship. As an allusion, I am going to use the relationship between a husband and wife. When a man and a woman get married, it takes time for both to know each other. During the marriage, they must spend time together to discover what the partner appreciates or despises. Before long, they get to a point where each person involved knows what pleases and displeases their spouse, and it is a continual process; so, it is with knowing the Father: we must spend time with Him and Him alone. We must desire to learn what He wants us to do and what is not in His will for us. In other words, set aside time from your busy schedule to fellowship with your Maker. Communicate with Him through prayer, learn of Him by reading your Bible, and walking with Him in obedience. These things we can achieve anywhere, anytime, and any place. We must remember that worship is not a seasonal thing but a lifetime journey until we see Him face to face, so take your time and love on Him. This is expressed in Joshua 1:8:

> This Book of the Law shall not depart from your mouth, but you shall meditate in it day and night, that you may observe to do according to all that is written in it. For then you will make your way prosperous, and then you will have good success. (Joshua 1:8 – NKJV).

Think of a couple who are in love. They create nicknames for each other as they grow up together. Sometimes, they may even have secret names that refer to things that have happened to them or for what one of them may have done. It is the same as when you get to know God through the Word of God and by the revelation of the Holy Spirit; your worship to Him must become something personal, where God becomes a personal God, where you make up names for Him like, my "tears wiper," my "secret keeper." You continue to build up from there; soon, you will have a worship vocabulary birthed from intimacy with God. It is our private worship that inspires our public worship. Knowing our Heavenly Father gives us the courage to talk about Him, live out loud, and have fellowship with Him.

Private or personal worship is when you spend time with your Heavenly Father to learn about Him through His Word, to understand His incredible love for us and how He wants us to worship Him.

> O God, You are my God; Early will I seek You; My soul thirsts for You; My flesh longs for You in a dry and thirsty land where there is no water. Because Your loving kindness is better than life, My lips shall praise You (Psalm 63:1,3 – NKJV).

These scriptures explain the psalmist's desire to be intimate with the Lord in worship. We should all have this kind of desire, where there is a hunger and thirst that worldliness cannot quench.

Personal worship time is one-on-one time with your Maker. It is time spent seeking His face in prayer, studying His Word, expressing worship, having intimate encounters; the time you converse with the Father when no one is there but you and the Holy

Spirit. Personal worship will inspire your collective worship. During private worship time, destinies and true identities via the Word of God and the process of new growth begins; desires for worldly things fade away, and a hunger for righteousness and holiness develops. When we set our worship right, then corporate worship becomes easy. When we commune with the Father during our worship time, we get to know Him, heightening our spiritual senses, allowing us to sense Him. Personal worship time makes the job easy for the worship team in our churches because the believer who spends time with their Father in secret can efficiently respond to Him in public and see worship as what it truly is—as unto God and not for the team. People will be more responsive during worship time; members will stop being disobedient to simple spiritual directions, such as, lift your hands, clap your hands, etc. One would always be ready to express worship no matter where they are because it is in the presence of God that the soul of a man begins to be transformed.

Corporate Worship

> Not forsaking the assembling of ourselves together, as is the manner of some, but exhorting one another, and so much the more as you see the Day approaching. (Hebrews 10:25 – NKJV).

> Speaking to one another in psalms and hymns and spiritual songs, singing and making melody in your heart to the Lord, giving thanks always for all things to God the Father in the name of our Lord Jesus Christ. (Ephesians 5:19-20 – NKJV).

Corporate worship is when the saints gather to worship; the children of God gather during weekday services or on Sundays for a celebration service. During these services, the saints of God sing and worship the Lord, share testimonies, and listen to the message for the day. During these services, a section is allotted for songs, hymns, and spiritual songs. It could run from fifteen to thirty minutes; those sections, as we all know, are categorically called "Praise and Worship" time, and it does not embody the totality of worship; those fifteen to forty-five minutes slot in our program during our services is a time through which we express our reverence, adoration, exaltation, and thanksgiving. Yes, it is an opportunity given to us to express ourselves as a family: the body of Christ. The totality of worship is living a life with the consciousness that we do not belong to ourselves, but we belong to our Maker and live for Him, so we must do everything to please Him in all that we do.

Once we become a part of the Kingdom of God, we have a desire to pursue God; discover our identity in Christ; we then take retrospect on how Jesus reached down and saved us from the most bottomless pit. Gratitude should fill our hearts, and we should be shouting.

Finally, worship is a way of life. Songs, hymns, spiritual songs, liturgical dance, and spoken words help us express how we feel about our Father. In corporate worship services, we sing to one another, share our victories, edify one another, receive healing, receive deliverance, and much more. We express how grateful we are by the way we worship.

Chapter Three

THE MINISTRY OF PRAISE AND WORSHIP

Besides the private or personal time of worship and corporate worship, there are those whom God has called, anointed, equipped, and commissioned to work in the ministry of praise and worship. They lead His people in praise and worship and stand on the frontline during praise and worship. The praise and worship leaders form part of the music ministry of a church; they should be skilled and knowledgeable about their responsibility. They are anointed as music ministers and can later be ordained as worship pastors. Music ministers lead and are also responsible for cultivating their relationship with the Father, participate in corporate worship, and know the mind of the Spirit for every service.

Skill, Knowledge, And Wisdom

To be skillful is to have knowledge and command over a given subject matter. For example, Chenaniah, the head of the Levites, oversaw the singing; it became his responsibility because he was skillful. He was also the instructor of music or the music director. (See 1 Chronicles 15:22). Likewise, every person in the worship ministry must strive to develop their God-given gift.

No matter the size of the congregation or the time allotted for praise and worship during a given service, we are to minister skillfully to the Lord and draw His precious children into His presence.

> Praise the Lord with harp: sing unto Him with the psaltery and an instrument of ten strings. Sing unto Him a new song; play skillfully with a loud noise. (Psalm 33:2-3 – KJV).

If you are in the music ministry, you must seek to "sharpen your gift," meaning, invest time and develop your gift. Do all you can to improve yourself with hard work and dedication, all of which require commitment. There are some things the Father will do through the manifest presence of His Holy Spirit. He is responsible for what we cannot do spiritually, and as music ministers, we are responsible for executing our assignment with excellence, grace, and knowledge by doing all we can do physically. We must be worthy of the Master's use at all times, as stated in the book of Timothy: *"Do your best to present yourself to God as one approved, a worker who does not need to be ashamed and who correctly handles the word of truth." (2 Timothy 2:15 – NIV).*

We must study the subject matter to have a command in our area of calling. We are born in an era where things evolve and knowledge is increasing. We cannot permanently hide behind the Holy Spirit to cover up our lack of knowledge and dedication; it always limits the ability to soar in the spirit. We do not neglect the fact that the Holy Spirit is the ultimate leader; we follow Him, and He leads us, He touches God's people and makes a change; in the same way, we must strive to create a worship atmosphere that is welcoming and embracing. As worship leaders, we cannot sing the same songs every Sunday, sing out of tune, make noise with our instruments, and yet expect Him to move because He chose to touch lives despite our limitations.

It will require teamwork, skillfulness, and continual growth to see a more significant move of God in our services. We must learn to add value to what we have and create beautiful melodies, allowing the Holy Spirit to change more lives by what we do. You may have entered the worship ministry with little knowledge, but you must decide to grow and learn all that you can to prepare yourself for the future. You must first ask yourself if leading worship is your calling. If you are persuaded, then go to school if you must. I would recommend that you learn to play an instrument, as it helps when no one is around to play for you.

Study the Word of God, pray and let the Holy Spirit use you. The more you advance yourself in your field, the more the Holy Spirit will use you. "Sharpening your gift" will permit you to serve on platforms of diverse audiences. However, be careful not to be complacent in your service to the Lord. You serve a God of excellence, and every leader should desire to grow to meet the need of the audience God has assigned you to serve. We must always be ready; our worship leading must transcend the boundaries of cultures and borders. If you serve a bilingual congregation, your worship has to meet the needs of everyone you serve. Be sensitive to the needs of the culture of your church.

> Wisdom is the principal thing; therefore, get wisdom: and with all thy getting get understanding. (Proverbs 4:7 – KJV).

Wisdom is the use of knowledge and understanding; we must spend time acquiring knowledge and then applying this knowledge in worship. We must be knowledgeable of our calling and use the knowledge we receive for the glory of God. Knowledge can sometimes puff up; that is why we need to get wisdom, "the know-how." Wisdom will guide us on how to use the knowledge gained. As worship leaders, we must appropriate the knowledge gained. We, as worship leaders, have to be on the cutting edge of the biblical foundation of worship—we can only give what we have.

Being knowledgeable and understanding who our Father is, builds us up, making each of us into better worship leaders. There are no two ways about it: there is no way we can lead someone to the throne room of God if we have no understanding of who God is. Our spiritual leaders, pastors, mentors, etc., can do a great job imparting this understanding into our lives, but you must have self-knowledge of who God is, which you can only find through intimacy with God. It is during your quiet time with God that you get to know Him personally; through prayer, He reveals Himself to us. Your worship hour is so important; it is when you are well-equipped that you grow in the knowledge of Him and see Him as He is.

Another essential part of growth as a worship leader is Word study. Everything you need to know is in the Word of God. You can find everything you need to know about your life, destiny, and how to become an effective worship leader in the Word of God. The Word of God is a manual for life; it is full of excellent spiritual information for life: *"For whatsoever things were written aforetime were written for our learning, that we through patience and comfort of the scriptures might have hope." (Romans 15:4 – KJV)*.

There are the fathers of faith, men and women who came before you, people God entrusted with a great anointing to blaze a trail for others to follow. Read about them, their work, and observe how they allowed the Holy Spirit to use them. Today, their works and lives are still being studied and referenced as people who change the scope of praise and worship. You can read books, attend workshops, attend conferences, but remember that the Word of God is the ultimate balance.

Godly Character

> Now the Berean Jews were of more noble character than those in Thessalonica, for they received the message with great eagerness and examined the Scriptures every day…. (Acts 17:11 – NIV).

No matter the role you play in church, be it ushering or cleaning, it is imperative to govern your life according to God's Word. Character is so important in the life of a believer because a worship leader's life is like an open book. As a worship leader, people may look up to you, admire you, hate you, and even want to be like you. Keep in mind that your character precedes your gifts. You are to be a representative of Christ onstage and offstage. You must practice what you sing; to exhibit ungodly character can destroy trust and hinder a believer from receiving from the Lord.

> Who may abide in Your tabernacle? Who may dwell in Your holy hill? He who walks uprightly and works righteousness and speaks the truth in his heart; he who does not backbite with his tongue, nor does evil to his

neighbor, nor does he take up a reproach against his friend. (Psalm 15:1-3 – NKJV).

Things that we consider trivial, like covering up a lie in our hearts, can be a great hindrance to true worship.

One may argue that believers ought to worship the Father and not concentrate on the lifestyle of a fellow believer; the truth is that the life of a believer is a living epistle. Your behavior tells a story about your walk with the Lord, and it can have a significant impact on a person. Remember, you lead God's precious ones in worship, and the expectation is high. As much as you do not live to please man, always live to please God; a double standard life can be a stumbling block.

The Holy Spirit, The Helper

But the Helper, the Holy Spirit, whom the Father will send in my name, He will teach you all things, and bring to your remembrance all things that I said to you. (John 14:26 – NKJV).

The Holy Spirit is your Helper; He is your teacher and the Companion of all believers. The Father has a purpose and plan for every service. He helps our weaknesses and strengthens us when we are tired; He comforts us during a challenging time in our ministry. The Holy Spirit is everywhere and has no limit. He is part of the Godhead, our Teacher, the one who reveals the mind and the deep things of God for any occasion.

As a worship leader, you must learn to walk by the leading of the Holy Spirit. The Spirit of God will help you avoid pitfalls in ministry; He can teach you how to lead any congregation into worship. When the Holy Spirit speaks, He speaks the will of God.

He is the source of strength, and He helps in all facets of worship leading, including song choice and songwriting. When God called you to this ministry, He laid His hands on you and gave you everything you would ever need to succeed. The Holy Spirit is our guide, and He is the one who tells us when a person is about to be healed while worshipping.

He Convicts Of Sin

When the Holy Spirit is present in our midst, He convicts us of sin by showing our flaws, faults, and mistakes lovingly and provides a way of escape. He has the power to show you what God wants you to work on or let go of in your character so you can become a better worshipper. He does it without condemnation, without pointing a finger, leaving you with a desire to do what is right, and He helps you to walk in obedience to the Word of God. He brings you to that place of repentance, but you have to be willing to turn away from those things that hinder your growth as a believer and ultimately as a worship leader.

> When he comes, he will prove the world to be in the wrong about sin and righteousness and judgment. (John 16:8 – NIV).

31

He Glorifies Jesus

All flesh should submit to the authority and Lordship of Jesus Christ. The Spirit of God was sent to help see and accept Christ as Lord. As such, your focus should go beyond the beautiful voices, well-articulated services, and gifted musicians. Jesus becomes your only desire, and you can worship freely. The flesh cannot please God, but you can offer authentic, pure worship with the help of the Holy Spirit.

Obedience Is Key

When you learn how to walk by the Spirit of God, it is equally essential to obey His Word. Walking by the Spirit of God should humble you, and you should become more flexible in the hands of God. If we follow Him and allow Him to interrupt our services, week after week, we will experience a move of God like never before. The Spirit of God is mighty; He enables you to minister through songs with great anointing, under the mighty hand of God. Obedience is an expression of our love for God, and worship cannot be true until you see obedience as an expression of love; if not, your worship will only be head knowledge. *"You are My friends if you do whatever I command you." (John 15:14 – NKJV).*

In Gerrit Gustafson's booklet "BE A BETTER WORSHIPPER," He talks about worship leadership as a place of service, and he also gave some great tips for leading worship.

The Worship Team As A Servant

Often, there is confusion about what precisely the worship team should be doing: are they supposed to be performing, or are they supposed to be leading worship?

There is undoubtedly a performance element to worship leading—a good performer is not self-conscious, neither should the worship team be uncertain about leading worship. There is a vast difference between the motivation of good worship leaders and what is commonly associated with the performer.

The worship leader's motivation should be like that of a butler, whose job is to escort the guest to the master's house. A performer's motivation would be to focus the attention of the guest upon his performance.

At the end of the booklet, there is a section on consecration. He explains how important it is for Worship teams to formally set time apart for the service of worship leading. Ask God to search your heart for wrong motivations and to prepare you for the highest privilege imaginable: serving in His house.

Worship Leading Tips

A worship leader is not just a "song leader." A song leader is happy if the song goes well. A worship leader, however, is looking for something more. He wants to see the song assist the people of God in coming into His presence, for there is where lives are healed, insight is given, and gifts are activated.

33

The "flow of the Spirit" is a key concept in the skill of leading worship. Be careful of abrupt, unnatural changes. Work on developing a "flow" with regard to the "feel" of the songs, the theme of the songs, and the songs' keys. Various patterns are helpful:

1) Thanksgiving, praise and, worship.
2) Outer court, holy place, holiest of all.
3) Celebration, adoration, and revelation.
4) Eventually, a worship leader will develop their own Spirit-inspired sense of the progression of songs.

Make sure your "Song Vocabulary" is always growing. Always be listening for good songs and different ways to minister songs you already know.

Culture

I have been privileged to live and work in different countries. I observed the way they interact with the elders. For example, the Yoruba tribe of Nigeria greets their elders with honor. When greeting an elder, the male prostrates, stays in that position until the elder, in return, greets and places a hand on the back of the greeter. The female will kneel and wait for a similar returned greeting. This act of greeting makes it easy for a believer of the Yoruba tribe to prostrate in the presence of God. On the contrary, a person of American decent will need to learn this aspect of worship before they consider prostrating in the presence of God simply because this is not part of their culture.

Your upbringing can also play a role in how you respond to worship. If you grew up in a home of royalty having servants when you become born again, you must renew your mind; otherwise, it will make no sense as to why you should prostrate in God's presence. Sometimes, a figure of authority may find it hard to obey simple instructions from the pulpit because they give orders and take orders from no one. If you are rebellious at home and find it difficult to obey your parents at home, it will be challenging to adhere to simple instructions from the pulpit simply because you are used to having your way. Some people have a strong will and a bad attitude because they are used to doing things the way they want to, when they want to, and how they want to. Some people lack knowledge or may be ignorant of the truth. Believers come with all the above issues to the body of Christ, and it takes a renewed mind and a humble heart to worship our Father, whom we do not see all the time. This means you, as a worship leader, must start by obeying the authority figures God has placed over you, no matter who they are or whether or not you like them.

The next time you are in service, be humble and obedient in following spiritual instructions.

Chapter 10 in this book includes many Hebrew and Greek words to help enhance your worship vocabulary and can be used as a guide for many years to come.

Chapter Four

DIFFERENT KINDS OF WORSHIP

Unbiblical Worship

Idol Worship

> When the people saw that Moses was so long in coming down from the mountain, they gathered around Aaron and said, "Come, make us gods who will go before us. As for this fellow Moses who brought us up out of Egypt, we don't know what has happened to him…" So all the people took off their earrings and brought them to Aaron. He took what they handed him and made it into an idol cast in the shape of a calf, fashioning it with a tool. Then they said, "These are your gods, Israel, who brought you up out of Egypt." (Exodus 32:1,3 – NIV).

The children of Israel were always rebellious by worshipping idols; likewise, we, as urban worshippers, can put things and people in place of God if we do not heed. This will make our worship ineffective. Before God brought the children of Israel out of Egypt with a mighty hand, He had made His intention known by giving Moses prophetic directions. God wanted His people, His chosen ones, to worship Him and no other gods. Instead, right after they left the house of bondage, while Moses stayed on the mount for further instructions and guidelines to live by, the Israelites' hearts turned to idol worship.

Idol worship is when something or someone is revered or placed first in a believer's life other than God. It occurs when man's heart places affection on material things or a person, and that thing or person is highly esteemed than God. Examples of these idols could be money, any material thing, spouses. Idol worship draws our attention to the creature rather than the creator.

Baseless Worship

When we do not know who we are worshipping, our worship is baseless because it has no object of worship.

> Then Paul stood in the midst of the Areopagus and said, "Men of Athens, I perceive that in all things you are very religious; for as I was passing through and considering the objects of your worship, I even found an altar with this inscription: TO THE UNKNOWN GOD. Therefore, the One whom you worship without knowing, Him I proclaim to you." (Acts 17:22-23 – NKJV).

While Paul was on one of his missionary journeys, he visited the inhabitants of Athens, who practiced polytheism. Paul noticed that they even had a space for a god they did not even know. This is the kind of worship I would call baseless worship that leads to eternal condemnation. For a person to not believe in the true and living God but believes in a god they do not know is scary. This kind of worship is filled with confusion and without foundational truth. In this account of rich biblical history, Paul used this as a perfect opportunity to preach the Gospel of Jesus Christ and win souls for the Kingdom of God.

Worship In The Flesh

> The Lord Says: 'These people draw near to Me with their mouth and honor me with their lips, but their hearts are far from me. Their worship of me is based on merely human rules they have been taught.' (Isaiah 29:13 – NIV).

This kind of worship is geared towards pleasing men instead of pleasing God. It is filled with arrogance and pride; it is self-seeking and hypocritical. This kind of worship is only to flaunt oneself and not glorify God. Whenever worshippers are engaged in this kind of worship, the Spirit of God will be unable to move; therefore, we lack the presence of God and prevent the release of God's power. Whenever we worship in the flesh, we show our concern is only for achievements instead of the souls of men, and we lack the ability to lead God's people into His presence.

True Worship

> But the hour is coming, and now is, when the true worshipers will worship the Father in spirit and truth; for the Father is seeking such to worship Him. God is Spirit, and those who worship Him must worship in spirit and truth. (John 4:23-24 – NKJV).

True worship has one focus: to please God. When God's people worship in spirit and in truth, there is such a harmony between the Spirit of God and His people that words cannot describe. God's people must come together with one heart and with one objective to please God in psalms, hymns, and spiritual songs. The music is captivating because the musicians are there to play in the spirit; the congregation is willing to go along for the ride, the worship leaders have such a reverence of God—they will do nothing to sabotage the love of God. True worship is scriptural, and it follows biblical principles.

There are many other kinds of worship that we will not focus on in this book, like New Age worship, traditional worship, animalistic worship, Satanic worship, etc., because I would like us to spend more time cultivating true worship.

Chapter Five

PRAISE

Praise means to commend, to applaud, to approbate for personal worth or actions. It also means to express in words or songs; to magnify; to glorify on account of perfection or excellent works. We are to speak of His goodness; ascribe all praises to Him, for He created us to offer praises to Him. Praise is an expression of a grateful heart. To praise is to make known His glory and excellent greatness, expressing our gratitude for the things He has done for us, speaking of His miraculous deeds, and only for the simple reason that He deserves our praise because He is God. We offer praise because we are God's creation, and as long as we breathe, we must give Him what is due to Him. We praise because it is a magnificent way to express our love for our Father, to sing out loud, and tell the world that our Father is the only true and living God.

> But ye are a chosen generation, a royal priesthood, a holy nation, a peculiar people; that ye should show forth the praises of Him who hath called you out of darkness into His marvelous light. (1 Peter 2:9 – KJV).

We have been chosen to exude with praises onto God; He created us with such abilities to move Him with our praise and worship. *"Let everything that hath breath praise the Lord." (Psalm 150:6a – KJV).* Praise is the expression of gratitude for personal favors conferred; a glorifying or extolling statement, an inkling of gratefulness for God's grace and mercy toward you, and as long as you can exhale and inhale, it is your biblical responsibility to offer

praise unto God, not just for His blessings but also for deliverance as shown in the Psalm 40:2-3.

> I will praise You with my whole heart; Before the gods I will sing praises to You. I will worship toward Your holy temple and praise Your name. (Psalm 138:1-2a – NKJV).

The Seven Hebrew Words That Describe Praise

1. **"Hallah"** is the most common word for praise.

> You shall eat in plenty and be satisfied, and praise the name of the Lord your God, who has dealt wondrously with you; and My people shall never be put to shame. (Joel 2:26 - NKJV).

> Praise the Lord! Praise God in His sanctuary; Praise Him in His mighty firmament! Praise Him for His mighty acts; Praise Him according to His excellent greatness! Praise Him with the sound of the trumpet; Praise Him with the lute and harp! Praise Him with the timbrel and dance; praise Him with stringed

instruments and flutes! Praise Him with loud cymbals; praise Him with clashing cymbals! Let everything that has breath praise the Lord. Praise the Lord! (Psalm 150:1-6 - NKJV).

According to Dr. Rogers' article on praise, "This word simply means to boast, brag, or rave about God even to the point of appearing foolish. People who attend football games often shout and scream and holler for their favorite team. They are called fans. Unfortunately, for most of us, if we shout and scream and brag on God, we may be labeled as fanatics - as if something is wrong with us."

Because your love is better than life, my lips will glorify you. I will praise you as long as I live, and in your name I will lift up my hands. (Psalm 63:3-4 - NIV).

And when the builders laid the foundation of the temple of the Lord, they set the priests in their apparel with trumpets, and the Levites the sons of Asaph with cymbals, to praise the Lord, after the ordinance of David king of Israel. And they sang together by course in praising and giving thanks unto the Lord because He is good, for His mercy endureth for ever toward Israel. And all the people shouted with a great shout, when they praised the Lord because the foundation of the house of the Lord was laid. (Ezra 3:10-11 - KJV).

After they laid the foundation of the Temple of the Lord, the people shouted. Praise is an avenue, a channel through which we make our boast in the Lord, show how proud we are to be His own, speak of His accomplishments, and say His ability is more than we expect. Our speech should be with enthusiasm, speaking with confidence about the things He has done, the things He is doing right now, and the things He will do.

Our voices should be loud and emotional about God. Praise gives us unhindered access to the throneroom of God. The Israelites shouted with such a loud voice that they could be heard from afar off. Praise is not a quiet thing. As we praise God, there must be such exuberance, such energy that is reflective of God's goodness and His ability to do the impossible.

The children of Israel had been with a temple, a place of worship for a while. There was also a generation that did not see the first temple King Solomon built. This event was a perfect opportunity for them to see how to live the stories told to them by their forefathers. They could go up to the Temple and participate in the offering of sacrifices, and when they saw the foundation of the Temple, not the finished building, but only the foundation, they began to brag, rave and boast of the handiwork of Jehovah. Therefore, we do not wait for the testimony to be complete, or we do not have to see the physical manifestation before we praise God. Like the children of Israel during the time of prophet Ezra, we ought to praise God for the little we have seen Him do while we are waiting for the miracle. Praise is an expression of your faith in God, that you are confident God will do what He has promised you.

2. **"Yadah"** means to worship with extended hands.

> Lift up your hands in the sanctuary and praise the Lord. (Psalm 134:2 - NIV).

> Why art thou cast down, O my soul? And why art thou disquieted within me? Hope in God: for I shall yet praise him, who is the health of my countenance, and my God. (Psalm 43:5 - KJV).

Yadah depicts a three-year-old child, hands raised, running toward daddy, crying, "Hold me, daddy, hold me!" Yadah is often translated as "giving thanks." Yadah is often a cry for help. Yadah praise is used when we are in desperate straits and need a victory from the Lord. Raising your hands is one of the most explosive and meaningful expressions of praise. Raising your hands is an international sign of surrender. A worshiping person raises hands in adoration and surrenders to God. It is refreshing to see that the lifting of hands during worship is biblical.

When we look through the scriptures, we will notice that people in the early days of the Bible raised their hands to praise our heavenly Father for various reasons; similarly, believers should shamelessly praise God and raise their hands before God.

Leah was Laban's eldest daughter and Jacob's most despised wife, but she was more fruitful than Rebecca. After giving birth to her husband's fourth son, she raised her hands in praise. She praised Him, for she believed that her husband would look upon her with love. Thus, Judah turned out to be a leader among His brothers and became an ancestor in the lineage of Jesus.

And she conceived again, and bare a son: and she said, Now will I praise the Lord: therefore, she called his name Judah; and left bearing. (Genesis 29:35 - KJV).

Judah, thou art he whom thy brethren shall praise: thy hand shall be in the neck of thine enemies; thy father's children shall bow down before thee. (Genesis 49:8 - KJV).

3. **"BARAK"** is used to denote blessing.

Barak hinted at the transcendent privilege of blessing the Lord. The book of Job in the Bible is one of the most popular accounts in the Bible of divine recovery. Job had experienced a significant loss. He lost family members, loved ones in a day; then he lost the trust of his friends in a couple of days; his wife told him to curse God and die. Job, though in great distress and loneliness, found a way in His heart to still praise the name of the Lord. His faith was questioned, his friends became judges, and his wife became a bad adviser and partner. She would rather see Job dead than see him suffer; she would rather see Job cursed by his Creator than stand by him and keep her vow to him "In sickness and in health." Job still praised God. He came to the place where he realized that earthly things are vanity, money has wings, and he had done everything in his power to prevent this tragedy, but it still occurred. He was considered a righteous man by God's standards; by his strength, he felt helpless; yet saw God as He is. Job did not let his current condition dictate how he praised God. He blessed the Lord in tribulation.

As believers, we ought to have the attitude of Job; bless the Lord when things are going right, when we have multiple testimonies, going through a wilderness period, experiencing the loss of a loved one, friend, or when all hope is lost. We praise Him during troubled times and diverse temptations because we have this confidence that if God put testimonies in our mouths before the mishap, He still has the power to do it again. He can revive His miraculous works amongst the children of men if He chooses to. But, if He does not, He does not become less than who He is: "The true and living God."

Scriptures tell us, *"John answered and said, A man can receive nothing, except it be given him from heaven." (John 3:27 - KJV).*

And said, Naked came I out of my mother's womb, and naked shall I return thither: the Lord gave, and the Lord hath taken away; blessed be the name of the Lord. (Job 1:21 - KJV).

We have a God who is a battle strategist. The children of Israel found themselves in captivity again. God spoke of their deliverance through His servant Deborah, who became a warfare partner with Barak. After their victory over their captors, they began to bless— Barak—the name of the Lord for delivering them from captivity. There was a jubilee among the children of Israel that day, and for a season, they remembered that men went to war, but God gave them victory. They did not forget to give glory to God.

As praise and worshippers, we must never forget to bless the name of the Lord for the victories we gain and the battles we have lost because He is worthy of praise and adoration in good times and bad times. What an awesome God He is!

Then sang Deborah and Barak the son of Abinoam on that day, saying, Praise ye the Lord for the avenging of Israel, when the people willingly offered themselves. (Judges 5:1-2 – KJV).

4. **"Tehillah"** means to sing or to laud.

Tehillah involves music and singing—especially singing. Singing is vital to the worship of God. There are over 300 Bible mandates to sing. This word suggests that God Himself is a song of praise. We might say it like this, "God is our song." God dwells and takes His position in the shouts and exuberant rejoicing of His people.

> But thou art holy, O thou that inhabitest the praises of Israel. (Psalm 22:3 - KJV).

This verse speaks of the coming of Jesus and how humanity will forsake Him. Matthew 27:46 writes, *"And about the ninth hour Jesus cried out with a loud voice, saying, Eli, Eli, lama sabachthani? that is, My God, My God, why have You forsaken Me?" (KJV).* During the time of Jesus' ministry here on earth, He endured many things, but it was the first time He felt like the Father forsook Him on the cross. Our praise should be even louder than our bleak situation. Tehilah is the kind of praise that draws God's attention—when we allow our praise to shoot beyond our troubles, faith arises, strength is released, and assurance is given. Before you know it, there will be a breakthrough. What a joy it is to see the Lord's face and to experience His presence when His children praise Him.

When we TEHILLAH, we sing a new song unto the Lord; our praise ascends to heaven, heavenly melodies are released, our praise becomes a beautiful sound that is birthed from the throneroom of

God, and no one has heard of it. It is raw praise; God is the engineer and the producer of the Tehillah sound. We get to experience a glimpse of how praise and worship will be: unrehearsed, uncensored, and yet full of the Spirit. We can learn valuable lessons from the Psalmist David. He played, wrote, and sang about almost everything in his life. God-Abba Father called him "A man after My own heart."

> And when he had removed him, he raised unto them David to be their king; to whom also he gave testimony, and said, I have found David the son of Jesse, a man after my own heart, which shall fulfill all my will. (Acts 13:22 - KJV).

> But now thy kingdom shall not continue: the Lord hath sought him a man after his own heart, and the Lord hath commanded him to be captain over his people, because thou hast not kept that which the Lord commanded thee. (1 Samuel 13:14 - KJV).

David was not a perfect man, but he understood how to praise God through the death of a beloved child, countless battles, victories, running for his life; today, we are benefactors of his boldness and his weakness as well.

Everyone who has a voice can sing a song unto the Lord; you do not need to have a great voice to worship your Father. He wants to hear from you. We sing the Lord's song because He is concerned about the little things in our lives. He strengthens us by His Holy Spirit and enables us to do what He requires of us.

The Lord is my strength and song, and he is become my salvation: he is my God, and I will prepare him an habitation; my father's God, and I will exalt him. (Exodus 15:2 - KJV).

Chapter Six

HEBREW WORDS FOR PRAISE

Zamar

"Zamar" means to pluck the strings of an instrument. Zamar speaks of rejoicing. It is involved with the joyful expression of music. Zamar means to sing praises or to touch the strings. It speaks of involving every available instrument to make music and harmony before the Lord. It is God's will that we be joyful. Use Zamar when you are rejoicing after God has done something great for you. Zamar is translated in the New Testament as "Psallo."

> Speaking to one another with psalms, hymns, and songs from the Spirit. Sing and make music from your heart to the Lord. (Ephesians 5:19 – NIV).

Music is such an essential part of our lives today. Hospitals, schools, and parents use music; and music is used as therapy for babies as well. One thing that separates Christian music from secular music is the Spirit of God. We play under the influence of the Spirit of God. He inspires us to play, and any gospel musician who is willing to obey the Spirit of God is on the path to allowing the Lord to use them powerfully.

David was skillful, humble, and anointed to play the harp. He played for his father's sheep; he played for King Saul, and most of all, he played and sang for an audience of one – God. David's relationship with God was evident when he played the harp. Deliverance took place in the life of King Saul when he played.

> And it came to pass, when the evil spirit from God was upon Saul, that David took an harp, and played with his hand: so, Saul was refreshed, and was well, and the evil spirit departed from him. (1 Samuel 16:23 = KJV).

David played when he was on the run for his life; when he lived in caves and strongholds; he played when all odds were against him. David played on his instrument any time, any place.

Instruments are a vital part of our worship, but the person who plays the instrument plays an essential role during worship. The Holy Spirit anoints the individual as they submit to Him, and the anointing of God flows through Him as He plays. Therefore, it is wise to stress the importance of consecration.

We have many skillful musicians out there who are knowledgeable but do not carry the unction to play for the heavens to open; they know but have not grasped the spiritual relevance of what they possess. Their playing is mere performance and entertainment. Skill is a great asset to a musician, but it is like a sounding gong if God cannot use your playing to heal or deliver a soul. Equally so, we have some musicians who understand the flow of the Spirit and operate under the unction of the Holy Spirit, but their ministration is limited to the little knowledge they have.

Believers must get to the place where we stop depending on the Spirit of God to do the work that He has empowered us to do. The phrase "We will flow with the Spirit or as the Spirit lead" has been taken out of context and used as a bargaining ticket for lack of excellence and preparation. Yes, the Spirit of God should always be in charge, and we should always follow His lead; we must do everything humanly possible and then let the Spirit of God lead us through our preparation. He will take over our agenda when He wants to. Let us not use these phrases to support our lack of excellence and preparation.

There must be a balance between the spiritual and physical. When we prepare, God can reveal His intentions for every given ministration. We must remember that our Father loves music; He is a God of excellence and deserves our best. So let us make some well-deserved investments in the gift that God has bestowed upon us.

We live in a busy-body age, a time when everything seems to be moving on steroids, where no one has the time to spend before the Lord. Consequently, we work in the realm of improvisation, pretending to be who we are not. I believe if we are going to see a revolution of true worship in our day and age, an army of radical praise and worshippers will have to rise, raise the bar, pay the price for the anointing, invest in prayer and fasting until the manifested presence of God changes lives during our sessions. The lives of the Psalmist David and the minstrel in 1st Kings chapter 3 are a constant inspiration. David and the minstrel did not have the Spirit of God living inside them, yet their worship produced much power and opened the Heavens. We have the Holy Spirit living inside of us; He is with us, and He comes upon us, yet the reception of man's approval clouds our meetings. We can neither see the glory cloud nor enter the Holy of Holies if we minister in the outer court. Worshipers should be asking, when we play and when we sing, how many people got saved, delivered, healed, and turned from their wicked ways?

If we are struggling to see the impact of God in the lives of individuals, how can we expect God to use our trumpet blowing and shouts to bring down the walls of Jericho? How can our music provoke change in the lives of those we minister to? When an anointed minister plays an instrument, there is an explosion. They both become one channel that the Spirit of God flows through. The heavenly melody that the Holy Spirit releases at that moment is interpreted by the person on the instrument. The Holy Spirit knows exactly what kind of sound needs to be produced for every given visitation of the Lord.

> I will love thee, O Lord, my strength. The Lord is my rock, and my fortress, and my deliverer; my God, my strength, in whom I will trust; my buckler, and the horn of my salvation, and my high tower. I will call upon the Lord, who is worthy to be praised: so shall I be saved from my enemies. (Psalm 18:1-3 - KJV).

David picked up his harp and began to praise God for deliverance by acknowledging Him, recognizing that it was the doing of the Lord and it was neither his strength nor his battle strategy. He reflected on his life both as a shepherd boy and the challenges he had faced, such as fighting a lion and a bear, facing rejection, facing Goliath, running for his life, sleeping in places that he never dreamt of (caves, stronghold), pretending to be insane to save his life, living in the enemy's territory, and losing the trust of his mighty men. Yet through all his life, David saw the hand of God orchestrating his escape and preserving his life. After God had given him rest from all his enemies, he began to play and sing as he reminisced upon God's faithfulness. Let this be an example of how we ought to be.

We should praise God in and out of season. Most of the time, we hold on until our change comes. Then, we turn our backs on the Lord and do not show our faces in church services until another problem arises. Praise requires consistency; we cannot praise our way through pain and do not acknowledge God, who gave us the solution. Believers, when you get your breakthrough, remember the Lord and give Him praise.

> Then he said to them, Go your way, eat the fat, drink the sweet, and send portions to those for whom nothing is prepared; for this day is holy to our Lord. Do not sorrow, for the joy of the Lord is your strength. (Nehemiah 8:10 - KJV).

> I will love You, O Lord, my strength. The Lord is my rock and my fortress and my deliverer; My God, my strength, in whom I will trust; My shield and the horn of my salvation, my stronghold. I will call upon the Lord, who is worthy to be praised; so shall I be saved from my enemies. The pangs of death surrounded me and the floods of ungodliness made me afraid. (Psalm 18:1-4 - NKJV).

Todah

"Todah" means to shout or to address with a loud voice. But Todah goes even further; it includes an attitude of gratitude for God's promised deliverance, even while we are still in need. This type of praise also refers to the lifting of the hands in inviting God's help. Todah praise is having faith and assurance that it is well even before the victory comes. For example, David, trapped by the Philistines in Gath. He gave thanks and offered Todah praise even before God delivered him.

> Be merciful to me, O God, for man would swallow me up; Fighting all day he oppresses me. My enemies would hound me all day, For there are many who fight against me, O Most High. (Psalm 56:1-2 - NKJV).

Todah praise is a kind of praise that stirs the devil in the face; it challenges the circumstance, the difficulty, and any situation that stands to defy God's ability to keep His promises. To offer "Todah Praise" means to offer praise regardless of your current state; it is a time that you reflect on past deliverance and draw strength and encouragement that He (God) is the same yesterday, today, and forever.

It is easy to celebrate when all is well, but Todah praise is needed when things are not well with us. We praise during these times because we cannot compare current challenges to the miracle-working power of our God. We can praise because we have the hope that all things will "work out for our good." Todah praise is the kind of praise that requires boldness, confidence, fearlessness, and faith.

Todah goes beyond tears, pains, discouragement, sickness, and any challenge. In Todah praise, we leave the place of doubt and enter the place of agreement with the promises of God's Word. We speak to our souls, reminding ourselves that our God is faithful: *"God is not a man, that he should lie; neither the son of man, that he should repent: hath he said, and shall he not do it? or hath he spoken, and shall he not make it good?" (Numbers 23:19 - KJV).*

When you genuinely offer up Todah Praise, it lifts your spirit, realigns your thoughts with the purpose of God, and in the end, God gets the glory. So, if you can stop focusing on the negative things around you and take your eyes off the magnifying glass of what your struggles are, you will experience such a great move of God like never before.

The lyrics of a Todah praise song become your confession because you proclaim God will turn things around through songs. Todah also means "Thanksgiving." 1 Thessalonians 5:18 reminds us to always offer thanksgiving in and out of season: *"In everything give thanks; for this is the will of God in Christ Jesus concerning you." (KJV).*

We see the result through the lenses of faith. After Todah praise, it is just a matter of time for a change. When a person offers Todah praise, it changes things. When sickness is present, the person speaks by faith that God can heal, putting you in the position to receive your healing by faith.

The story of Jonah is a popular account of one man's disobedience that left him in the belly of the fish, but it does not end there. Jonah realizes that he disobeyed; his disobedience led to his affliction; he began to cry out to God from the belly of the fish; God heard him when he decided to offer up a sacrifice of thanksgiving with his voice.

When we sacrifice or make a sacrifice, it shows an effort that goes above and beyond. Jonah, entangled in the fish belly, saw beyond his painful limitation, and after repentance, he began to praise God for his deliverance. Our God is merciful.

Todah praise denotes that we have a revelation that only God can bring us through. We lift our hands during this time and raise our "eyes unto the hills." It is praise that comes from the desperation of the soul unto the God who is able to bring deliverance. We are calculative and consciously making an extra effort to remind ourselves that it may be bleak right now, but my help is in the name of the Lord. I can trust His abilities to bring a solution, but until then, I will praise Him; I will shout for joy; I will lift my hands and give Him the sacrifice of praise. If we can stand in the position of praise, no odd position will be permanent.

As long as we serve the living God, things will change for the better. Jonah's case required a miracle—it is impossible to survive after being eaten by a fish. In the natural world, there is a possibility that Jonah would have died in the belly of the fish, and the fish would have been full for days until after the decay of Jonah's body. Without God's intervention, he was not going to see the daylight again; that would have been the end of Jonah's life and the completion of his assignment. Thank God for His "mercies that are renewed every morning" and His sovereignty.

We serve an omnipotent and omnipresent God. There is nothing impossible with Him. Think about it for a second; there is no guarantee that the fish would have been caught. Jonah had already stayed in the belly of the fish for three days. If Jonah had been rescued by man, it would have been by God's divine direction, instruction to man, and intervention. God would have given specific instructions about where the fish was, who would have caught it; Jonah knew better than to rely on the probability of the fisherman catching the fish; instead, he turned to the Creator of the fish and the only One able to speak to a fish and cause it to obey. You may think your situation is beyond what man can do, but God is still in the business of working miracles; your case is no different. If you can realize that you need help, turn your eyes toward God and give Him praise for the situation and for bringing you out. He can work miracles in your life.

> Then Jonah prayed unto the Lord his God out of the fish's belly, And said, I cried by reason of mine affliction unto the Lord, and he heard me; out of the belly of hell cried I, and thou heardest my voice. But I will sacrifice unto thee with the voice of thanksgiving; I will pay that that I have vowed. Salvation is of the Lord. And the Lord spake unto the fish, and it vomited out Jonah upon the dry land. (Jonah 2:1-2, 9-10 – KJV).

Chapter Seven

THE BENEFITS OF PRAISE AND WORSHIP

Praise: An invitation for God to dwell amongst His people with a physical manifestation.

But thou art holy, O thou that inhabitest the praises of Israel. (Psalm 22:3 – KJV).

God is omnipresent, which means He can be everywhere simultaneously through the precious Holy Spirit. Our praises do not dethrone God from heaven; instead, praise enthrones Him in our midst. He shows up and takes a seat, as we offer praises with a grateful heart. His presence is evident so that we mere men can identify that He particularly is with us. It is incredible how God responds to praise; God will always visit us in peculiar ways as long as we offer praise.

Praise Will Bring Deliverance

And at midnight Paul and Silas prayed, and sang praises unto God: and the prisoners heard them. And suddenly there was a great earthquake, so that the foundations of the prison were shaken: and

> immediately all the doors were opened, and every
> one's bands were loosed. (Acts 16:25-26 - KJV).

Praises will open prison doors and break the bands of any kind of bondage. When we look closely at this account in Acts chapter 16, we can see God's miraculous intervention firsthand as Paul and Silas prayed and offered praises. Two men were thrust into the inner prison for executing their assignment, and instead of grumbling or complaining, they found the courage to pray and praise. When Paul and Silas began to pray and praise God, the other prisoners heard them praying and praising; the prisoners had heard the good news of the Kingdom of God. They did not only listen to the gospel of Jesus Christ, but they also experienced the miraculous power of God firsthand, their chains broke loose, and they were set free. Praise will bring deliverance to you and those around you. It can provoke God's supernatural intervention.

Praise Will Give You Victory In Warfare

> And when he had consulted with the people, he
> appointed singers unto the Lord, and that should praise
> the beauty of holiness, as they went out before the
> army, and to say, Praise the Lord; for his mercy
> endureth forever. And when they began to sing and to
> praise, the Lord set ambushments against the children
> of Ammon, Moab, and mount Seir, which were come
> against Judah; and they were smitten. (2 Chronicles
> 20:21-22 - KJV).

The children of Judah praised the Lord in the face of significant opposition. They were outnumbered and did not have a large troop, but they prevailed by wisdom and divine providence. They entreated the Lord, and based on the Lord's instructions, they went out on the battlefield with songs of praise.

Praise will make you fearless.

This is a kind of praise that stares the opposition in the face and proclaims the goodness of God. We can sing praises during trouble because we have this great confidence that Abba Father, who is worthy of our praise, is well able to give us the victory.

Praise is not always in the absence of battle. If we can look beyond the thing that seems like a mountain and put our trust in the Lord, victory will be ours. Like the children of Judah and Jerusalem, what the enemy intended for evil, God turned it around for their good. God can turn the enemy's evil plans around for good, thus giving us victory. The mandate from hell and whatever opposes us can be changed when we offer praise in the face of difficult times. Praising during trials should be done with a mindset that God will bring you out. We offer praise during tribulation because we know that God is more significant than our problem, and He can give a solution.

Praise Will Cause Fruitfulness/ It Brings Down The Blessings Of God

> Let the people praise thee, O God; let all the people praise thee. Then shall the earth yield her increase; and God, even our own God, shall bless us. God shall bless us; and all the ends of the earth shall fear him. (Psalm 67:5-8 - KJV).

Our Father created our planet, and it responds to the Lord in a way only He understands. When we praise God, He blesses our world with fruitfulness. When the earth yields her increase, it means that the people will have all that they need. Everything on the earth produces to benefit the inhabitants. If there is a generation of radical praise and true worshippers, their praise and worship can provoke God to bless the land. Our praise and worship can release the blessings of God on our land. What a blessing it will be when we rise in praise! According to the above scripture, there will be abundant food, fewer sicknesses and diseases; provision will be available for all in high quantity with more than enough to share.

Praise Will Pave The Way For God's Shekinah Glory To Fall

> It came even to pass, as the trumpeters and singers were as one, to make one sound to be heard in praising and thanking the Lord; and when they lifted up their voice with the trumpets and cymbals and instruments of musick, and praised the Lord, saying, For he is good; for his mercy endureth for ever: that then the house was filled with a cloud, even the house of the Lord; So that the priests could not stand to minister by reason of the cloud: for the glory of the Lord had filled the house of God. (2 Chronicles 5:13-14 - KJV).

We have to understand that in the book of Leviticus, God was specific about the laws given, and everyone was required to abide by the law. The High Priest would enter the holy of holies just once a year to perform his duties by offering sacrifices to God on behalf of the children of Israel and his family. He never broke the protocol but carried out effectively every ritual leading up to the holy of holies. If the High Priest made a mistake in the holy of holies, he would die.

Now, after the trumpeters and singers sanctified themselves, they began to sing praises to God, and for once in the history of Israel, they did not need a priest to intercede for them. When they started to praise in one accord, their praises opened the heavens, and God responded with His Shekinah glory: His very presence. On that day, all protocols were broken; the One who gave the law was in town. It became a holiday for the priest on that day. Wow, Jesus is Lord! What a dimension to live in, where the fivefold ministry gifts become less burned because a praise and worship team are so sanctified and consecrated for the Lord to move freely. What a blessing it will be!

HINDRANCES TO EFFECTIVE PRAISE AND WORSHIP

Ignorance

We must understand that we cannot offer genuine praise and worship without understanding who God is. Once we come to Christ, we are babies in Christ.

> As newborn babes, desire the sincere milk of the word,
> that ye may grow thereby: If so be ye have tasted that
> the Lord is gracious. (1 Peter 2:2-3 – KJV).

However, we have a responsibility to grow from babyhood to becoming mature Christians, and this is equally important when we worship; worship requires knowledge and understanding. You cannot be passionate about a person you do not know, and you cannot worship with boldness. Likewise, worshippers cannot lead God's people in His presence if we do not know Him and don't have the right tools to lead worship effectively. We must prepare ourselves to lead worship if we want God to meet us. Knowledge is power. When you speak about a thing, a person you know, you speak with boldness, and the message you are conveying comes with confidence.

> The wicked flee though no one pursues, but the righteous are as bold as a lion. (Proverbs 28:1 - NIV).

Pride

It is very easy for a believer to become self-conceited and haughty. Every musician must strive to serve beyond pride because the scripture teaches us to esteem others more highly than ourselves.

> Do nothing out of selfish ambition or vain conceit. Rather, in humility value others above yourselves. (Philippians 2:3 - NIV).

Pride is the opposite of humility; no matter how much we believe God is using us or how He has used us, we must always keep ourselves abased and not become puffed up. We should never compare ourselves to others or think we are better because of our positions, size of our ministry, depth of understanding of praise and worship, or excellent execution of our assignment as praise and worshippers. Instead, we are to complement one another, support one another, and complete the work as a team in the body of Christ. We all worship one God, and the fact that you operate more in your gift than others does not put you in a higher place. God resists the proud and gives grace to the humble.

Carnality

A carnal Christian is a person who is born again but has confidence in the flesh. A carnal praise and worship leader has no sense of direction for a given service. Leading God's precious ones into His presence is a sacred calling; therefore, there should be no place to entertain the flesh. Every praise and worship leader must seek to be led by the Holy Spirit and submit to Him. He is the one who knows the mind of God, and He is the one who reveals the mind of God to us. He is our "Helper." God has an agenda; every time we gather to learn about Him, we as leaders must do everything possible to lead people according to the direction of the Holy Spirit. When we walk in the flesh, we become men-pleasers and self-achievers. Instead of a time of ministration, it becomes a performance, and performance will never get anyone into the presence of God.

We should keep in mind that when we perform to gratify the flesh, we are no different from those who have dedicated their lives to creating music that appeals only to the soulish desires of men. We minister for an audience of one, who is our Father. We must see ourselves as worshippers with the sole purpose of pleasing only our Father. There will be no deliverance or yoke breaking if we strive to please the flesh. Our meetings will produce a sounding gong effect without life transformation. Let us allow the Spirit of God to lead us in everything we do. It is His place; we are just the vessels God has chosen to use.

Prayerlessness

Prayer is simply communicating with our Father, and every believer must learn how to pray. Cultivating a life of prayer is crucial for any assignment, including leading praise and worship. Praise and worship leaders must include prayers for their calling, service, and daily prayer life. As the saying goes, "a prayerless Christian is a powerless Christian." We should not make it our habit of communicating with our Father only when there's a need. We have this great privilege to usher God's chosen ones before His throne. Instead, we should maintain an open line of communication regularly. When prayerful, you become more sensitive to what God wants to do in a given service.

Bringing God's people before His throne is a huge responsibility. If we ask in prayer, the Spirit of God will lead us. It will become a smooth ride into His presence if we look beyond our planned programs and allow Him to meet the need of His people. The early church understood the power of prayer, and God did miraculous things through them; even the Bible admonishes us to pray without ceasing. When the early church prayed, they prayed before going to work. Our perfect example is our Lord and Savior, Jesus Christ; no matter how long He worked during the day, He always went on the mountain to commune with God. Sometimes, we are so busy with spiritual activities that we neglect the most important things like prayer and meditation on the Word of God. We forget to feed our spirit. When we pray, we allow God to minister to us; we give Him access to refresh, restore, re-energize, strengthen us and fill us again and again to do His work. Thus, prayer is life to a believer, especially a minister.

Pray without ceasing (I Thessalonians 5:17 - KJV).

Worldliness

We must represent the Kingdom of God in every area of our lives, especially those of us who play a crucial role. We stand up on stage for most of our lives leading worship, so dress code is essential and we must not send mixed messages to our audience. When God set the order in the Old Testament for the priest, He was concerned about how they dressed and hid their undergarment. A female worship leader must dress with the consciousness that she will express herself in worship; therefore, she must cover her cleavage. Likewise, men must dress appropriately. We cannot copy the world and present it in a religious package with our craft then reintroduce it to the saints of God. Everything counts, including the way we dress.

Our bodies are the temple of the Holy Spirit. He dwells in us, and sadly, we have adopted the world's system, and we are carrying out their agenda. We cannot change the world if we still behave like we are in the world. We must become more mature even in the way we dress; transformation must be evident in our lives, holding on to the Word of God as our lifeline. Remember that our words, dress code, and character must align with God's Word and not like unbelievers.

> Do not conform to the pattern of this world, but be transformed by the renewing of your mind. Then you will be able to test and approve what God's will is— his good, pleasing and perfect will. (Romans 12:2 - NIV).

Sin

> My dear children, I write this to you so that you will not sin. But if anybody does sin, we have an advocate with the Father—Jesus Christ, the Righteous One. (1 John 2:1 - NIV).

We all fell short of God's glory, but provision for our sins is available by the death of Jesus Christ on the cross. If a worshipper decides to live in habitual sin, there is no way his/her worship will be pleasing to God. Therefore, we must do everything possible to keep our minds, hearts, and spirit in purity, giving glory to our Father in heaven.

Chapter Eight

PRAISE AND WORSHIP EXPRESSIONS

Free To Lift My Hands

Hand lifting should be no strange thing to us; it is an old-age practice since Biblical times. Lifting hands is a Biblical Christian tradition used during the time of prayer and worship. The Hebrew word for lifting hands is "Yadah," which means to use, hold out the hand, to throw a stone or arrow, at or away, to revere or worship, with extended hands, praise, thanksgiving.

> Praise the Lord with the harp; Make melody to Him with an instrument of ten strings. (Psalms 33:2 - NKJV).

> Therefore I will give thanks to you, O Lord, among the Gentiles, and sing praises to your name. (Psalms 18:49 - NKJV).

People have many reasons as to why hand lifting is a strange thing. We struggle to lift our hands because we sometimes feel embarrassed; some refuse to raise their hands because of a lack of understanding, pride, and rebellion. The scriptures should justify our reasons. If what we are doing (not lifting our hands in worship) contradicts the scriptures, then it is about time we repent and do what is right.

Culture, traditions, associations, and what I call the "monkey see, monkey do syndrome" stop us from obeying the scriptures.

Scriptures state: *"Thus will I bless thee while I live: I will lift up my hands in thy name." (Psalm 63:4 - KJV).*

> And Ezra blessed the Lord, the great God. Then all the people answered, "Amen, Amen!" while lifting up their hands. (Nehemiah 8:6a - NKJV).

> I will therefore that men pray everywhere, lifting up holy hands, without wrath and doubting. (1 Timothy 2:8 - KJV).

When we raise our hands in worship, it is a sign of reverence and surrender. When we lift our hands to the Lord in prayer or during praise and worship, it expresses reference and adoration. We raise our hands because we also know that our Father is beyond the skies, looking down on us, and our praise and worship are ascending as a sweet-smelling perfume. It may seem like a foolish thing to do, but it is scriptural—it was a practice of God's chosen people in Bible times.

> Lift up your hands in the sanctuary, and bless the LORD. (Psalm 134:2 - KJV).

> Let us lift up our hearts and our hands to God in heaven, and say: (Lamentations 3:41 - NIV).

Do not limit yourself. You can lift your hands in praise and when you are crying out to God for help in times of mercy.

> Hear the voice of my supplications when I cry to You, when I lift up my hands toward Your holy sanctuary. (Psalm 28:2 - NKJV).

Free To Kneel/Bow

Psalm 95:6 says: *"Oh come......let us kneel before the Lord our maker." (NKJV).*

To kneel means to bend the knee, to fall, or rest on the knees. "Kara" also means to bend, sink down to one's knees, to kneel in reverence. It is scriptural to fall on one's knees in worship,

> (for Solomon had made a bronze platform five cubits long, five cubits wide, and three cubits high, and had set it in the midst of the court; and he stood on it, knelt down on his knees before all the assembly of Israel, and spread out his hands toward heaven); and he said: "Lord God of Israel, there is no God in heaven or on earth like You, who keep Your covenant and mercy with Your servants who walk before You with all their hearts. (2 Chronicles 6:13-14 - KJV).

Regardless of your status in life, you must be humble to bow in God's presence and to offer true worship, just as King Solomon was not ashamed to express himself in praise and worship. Kneeling in

73

the presence of God is a biblical tradition, and it is no strange thing to kneel in God's presence. Kings and peasants knelt in God's presence. It is not a set place for the lower or upper class. We kneel in obedience to God during our prayer and to express our worship. We kneel to show our humility to the greatest God of all time, who happens to be our Father. We kneel in holy fear, respect, and reverence to an all-consuming God who is so merciful to us. As children of God, when knowledge is received, our mindset must be renewed, and we must lay down our pride. Kings, royalties, those in authority, lower-class—whoever you are—we have been given a command to kneel in the presence of the most high God, the God of all things.

Just as we lift our voices to sing a song of praise anytime, you can express worship everywhere and anywhere. Some may say that it is a practice of the Islamic religion but remember, Muslims pray five times a day, looking towards the sun, but not so with Christians. Whatever is backed by scriptures must be obeyed. So, if you are worshiping in public or in private, feel free to kneel in the presence of God; do not be a limited worshipper; in the Bible, people bowed and worshipped Jesus, but now we only express worship this way during the gathering of the saints.

Sometimes pride and social status can hinder the way we worship, and it should not be so. Music ministers cultivate the habit of worshipping anywhere, and every child of God is encouraged to do so as well. Worship will change you, and it will humble you when you see yourself as nothing in the eyes of God and realize that it is by the mercies of God that you are not consumed.

Free To Prostrate

If a man cannot kneel in the presence of God, he will never prostrate or bow in the presence of Jehovah, the Creator of the heavens and the earth, the Maker and former of our being. To prostrate is to lay down flat, with our face to the ground, in a sense, where we revere God, our Father, so much that we have this holy fear even to stand, sit, or kneel before Him. Reverence will bring holy fear and lead to one prostrating before their Maker. We worry about the clothes we have on, what people will think about us, what they will say, and we form a picture in our mind about the right way to worship. As a result, our worship has become pleasing to man and not pleasing to God. Psalm 95:6 says: *"Oh come......let us kneel before the Lord our maker." (NKJV)*.

Free To Clap

Clapping hands is associated with celebration, scorn, ridicule, warfare. We clap our hands during prayer and praise and worship as a sign of celebration and added instruments. The Bible shines a light on some of the reasons why clapping hands should be part of a believer's life.

> Oh, clap your hands, all you peoples! Shout to God with the voice of triumph! For the Lord Most High is awesome; He is a great King over all the earth. He will subdue the peoples under us, and the nations under our feet. (Psalm 47:1-3 – NKJV).

God instructed His people to rejoice and clap their hands because of the victory He had given them. Clapping in this scripture is

75

accompanied by shouts of joy. We use clapping hands during praise and worship as an added instrument that comes from a place of excitement, joy, peace, and expression of the goodness of God. While it is true that some people clap to keep rhythm, clapping hands, as shown in this scripture, goes far beyond that. When we praise the Lord and think about how He has caused us to overcome the enemy, it ought to make us clap victoriously. Clapping is synonymous with "applaud." To clap means to manifest approbation of praise or give approval. Clapping hands is an expression of celebrating the ability of God, our Father, to contend with the contender on our behalf. So, the next time you go to church and the praise and worship team encourages you to clap your hands, do not think it is strange.

Clapping of hands is also associated with warfare. In Psalm 47:1-3, the Hebrew word for clap means to strike, to thrust a weapon, or give a blow. So, use your hands in prayer to strike the enemy, send an impact, and thrust a weapon on the enemy, and as children of God, we should add clapping of hands to our praise, worship, and prayers; it is practical and scriptural.

Free To Dance

> Let them praise his name in the dance: let them sing praises unto him with the timbrel and harp. (Psalm 149:3 – KJV).

> You have turned for me my mourning into dancing; You have put off my sackcloth and clothed me with gladness. (Psalm 30:11 - NKJV).

Dancing has always been associated with rejoicing and giving praises in the Bible. This is a highly debated issue in the body of Christ. It is incredible when God's people express themselves through dance. Liturgical dance is becoming an acceptable way of worshipping God in the body of Christ. As a liturgical dancer, it has always been my prayer that God will use dancers to glorify His name and bring a breakthrough in the atmosphere for God's people to experience His glorious presence.

Now, one must keep in mind that as a child of God, anything and everything we do must be done to bring glory to the Father through Christ Jesus. 1 Corinthians 10:31b says: *"...whatsoever ye do, do all to the glory of God." (KJV)*. Dances are expressions of deep emotion, excitement, joy, and victory, as in the case of the children of Israel after God opened the Red Sea and saved them from the hands of Pharaoh and his army. Miriam and the women sang, played timbrels, danced, and praised God for the notable deliverance.

> Then Miriam the prophet, Aaron's sister, took a timbrel in her hand, and all the women followed her, with timbrels and dancing. (Exodus 15:20 – NIV).

Dances can be done in groups or alone. All churches may not have or accept the ministry of liturgical dance, but one must follow Biblical principles and Biblical standards for dancing in the house of God. We were created to show forth His glory even in dance. Therefore, if we have the Spirit of God living inside us, we should be able to dance before our King.

> Then David danced before the Lord with all his might;
> and David was wearing a linen ephod. (2 Samuel 6:14
> – NKJV).

Dance should have one audience, like worship. For example, David danced before the Lord and did not care about his position as king; he laid down his royal garment, and God was pleased with him to the point of making his wife barren because she scolded him. This tells us that God was pleased with David's dance. Therefore, dancing should be encouraged in churches, expressing ourselves with different moves as the Holy Spirit inspires us.

> When David returned home to bless his household,
> Michal daughter of Saul came out to meet him and
> said, "How the king of Israel has distinguished himself
> today, going around half-naked in full view of the
> slave girls of his servants as any vulgar fellow would!"
> David said to Michal, "It was before the Lord, who
> chose me rather than your father or anyone from his
> house when he appointed me ruler over the Lord's
> people Israel—I will celebrate before the Lord." (2
> Samuel 6:20-21 – NIV).

Be careful not to criticize a person when they are dancing before the Lord. If we read the preceding chapters, we will understand that David danced before the Lord because the Ark of the Covenant, the very presence of God, was being brought back to Israel. The presence of God was their confidence and covering. I believe that David understood what it was to be without the presence of God. He understood that a nation suffers without the presence of God.

I remembered many years ago, my sister and I were dancing to a song by the gospel group "Shekinah Glory" titled "Yes." As we danced and ministered to this song, the power of God felt like a covering, and we were moving our bodies as the Spirit of God wanted us to move. Our dance moves were synchronized and backed by the power of God. We felt like we had fire in our bones and the people of God were so blessed that they began to worship and yield their hearts to the Lord. God takes pleasure in our dance when it is from a pure vessel, and the intention is to bring God glory.

Provocative Dances, A Hindrance

Dances that prompt you to use certain protruding parts of your body are unscriptural. For example, dances that have overtaken the world are slowly creeping in the church, and the body of Christ must reject them. Liturgical dancers should seek the face of God and study scriptures for dance interpretations, and they must be properly attired. Lustful dances should not be encouraged in the church.

Traditional Dances

Traditional dances tell stories about the past, present, and sometimes things to come. Some traditional dances are used to invoke spirits; some are carried out for the departing souls and hail men. These dances are part of rituals and offering sacrifices to gods. You must be careful what moves you use to dance and what kind of dance you interpret.

Free To Shout

There are many reasons why a person shouts, but we will be addressing what is necessary for the sake of content. According to dictionary.com, to shout means "to speak or laugh noisily or unrestrainedly or a sudden loud outburst, as of laughter."

> Oh, clap your hands, all you peoples! Shout to God with the voice of triumph! (Psalm 47:1 – NKJV).

The Hebrew word for shout in this scripture is "RUA," which means to mar, especially by breaking—split the ears with a loud sound, to make a joyful noise.

> Cry out and shout, O inhabitant of Zion, for great is the Holy One of Israel in your midst! (Isaiah 12:6 – NKJV).

The Hebrew word "Ranan" means to cry aloud, make a joyful sound. There are times you cannot find the right words, moves, or gestures to express yourself in God's presence. Shouting is allowed, but it can distract and disrupt the service when it becomes overshadowing and done incorrectly. When the people shouted in scriptures during praise and worship, it was in unison, in groups or the nation of Israel. We shout during praise and worship or a time of warfare, as in the case of Joshua and the children of Israel at the wall of Jericho.

Free To Sing

Singing is an expression of our most profound joy and satisfaction. It is such a blessing to sing to the Lord and fellow believers.

Angels Singing Along:

> And they sing the song of Moses the servant of God, and the song of the Lamb, saying, Great and marvellous are thy works, Lord God Almighty; just and true are thy ways, thou King of saints. (Revelations 15:3 – KJV).

Angels do sing and sometimes accompany us in our worship, if God chooses to let them. I had a personal experience in 1997. We had traveled as a team to Lagos, Nigeria, and we were guests at a church to minister in songs. While singing, I heard instruments like cymbals and some other musical instruments I cannot describe; these made the song's melody sound beautiful. After the meeting, I asked my husband who were the other musicians who joined us on stage to assist, and he said no one joined us. I knew then that we had divine assistance during our ministration. The music was so pure, effortless, and graceful than what we usually hear.

In the book of Luke, the Word of God says: *"And suddenly there was with the angel a multitude of the heavenly host praising God and saying, 'Glory to God in the highest, and on earth peace among those with whom he is pleased!' When the angels went away from them into heaven, the shepherds said to one another, 'let us go over to Bethlehem and see this thing that has happened, which the Lord has made known to us.'"* (Luke 2:13-15 – NKJV).

81

Singing existed in heaven and even before God created men. Praise and worship have been going on for eternity. Our earthly worship is an extension and, really, just a glimpse of what heaven will be. This is the only religious activity that will continue in heaven. We have such an honor to taste and sometimes see how worship will be endless in heaven. Angels have perfect melody; they express themselves with joy as they sing. If singing is a good thing in heaven, it is expedient to express ourselves in singing.

Humanity Is Commanded To Sing Praises To God

> Let the message of Christ dwell among you richly as you teach and admonish one another with all wisdom through psalms, hymns, and songs from the Spirit, singing to God with gratitude in your hearts. (Colossians 3:16 - NIV).

A hymn is a song of praise, a song that honors God. A hymn can also be a song of thanksgiving to God. Hymns were an ancient practice of the believers when Jesus ate the last supper with His disciples; they sang a hymn. In Mark 14:26, after they had sung a hymn, they went out to the Mount of Olives. A hymn is sung corporately; singing hymns in services is Biblical, and as worshippers, we must be encouraged to add sound and scriptural hymns to our time of worship.

Psalms: the Hebrew meaning of the word Psalm is "praise." Spiritual songs are birthed in the hearts of believers by the Spirit of God. They may not always be songs of worship or praise, but also testimonial songs with scriptural meanings. We sing songs for different reasons; sometimes, we sing a victory song, such as Moses and the children of Israel after God gave them a great deliverance from the hands of Pharaoh.

> Then sang Moses and the children of Israel this song unto the LORD, and spake saying, I will sing unto the Lord for He had triumphed gloriously: the horse and his rider hath He thrown into the sea. (Exodus 15:1 – KJV).

We are to sing the praises of God among the unbelievers. Our praises to God amongst our unbelieving family members, friends, communities, and the world are ways of telling the world of the goodness of God. Psalms 18:49 says: *"Therefore will I give thanks unto thee, O Lord, among the heathen, and sing praises unto thy name." (KJV).*

Chapter Nine

RESOURCES

Greek Worship Words

Listed below are several Greek words related to praise and worship. This chapter also includes scripture references with the Greek word in bold.

Most of the Greek definitions have been compiled from Strong's Exhaustive Concordance of the Bible. We have taken the eight most prominent words and listed them first.

Agalliao: "Jump for joy, exult, be exceedingly glad, with exceeding joy, rejoice (greatly)." (Luke 10:21, Acts 16:34).

Kampto: "to bend." (Romans 14:11, Ephesians 3:14).

Humneo: "to hymn, religious ode, to celebrate God in song, sing a hymn, praise (unto)." (Matthew 26:30, Acts 16:25).

Humnos: "to celebrate, one of the psalms, hymn." (Ephesians 5:19, Colossians 3:16).

Oide: "a chant or ode (the general term for any words sung), song." (Colossians 3:16, Revelation 5:9).

Psalmos: "a set piece of music, a sacred ode accompanied with the voice, harp or other instruments." (1 Corinthians 14:26, Colossians 3:16).

Ado: "to sing." (Revelation 15:3).

Aineo: "to praise." (Luke 2:13, Luke 24:53, Acts 3:8).

Ainesis: "the act of praising, to thank." (Hebrews 13:15).

Ainos: "a story, praise." (Luke 18:43).

Allelouia: "praise ye Jehovah, an adoring exclamation." (Revelation 19:1, Revelation 19:4).

Arete: "manliness, excellence, praise, virtue." (1 Peter 2:9).

Chairo: "to be cheerful, happy or well off, God speed, hail, joy, rejoice." (Philippians 3:1, Philippians 4:4).

Choros: "a ring, round dance, choir, dancing." (Luke 15:25, Acts 6:5).

Note: Prochorus, one of the appointed deacons, means leader of the dance.

Doxa: "glory, dignity, honor, praise, worship." (Luke 2:14, 1 Peter 4:11).

Doxazo: "to render or esteem, glorious, honor, magnify, full of glory." (Luke 18:43, Revelation 15:4).

Enopion: "in the face of, before, in the presence (sight) of." (Luke 4:7).

Epaineo: "to applaud, commend, laud, praise." (Romans 15:11).

Epainos: "laudation, a commendable thing, praise." (Ephesians 1:12,14).

Ethelothreskeia: "voluntary, arbitrary and unwarranted piety, sanctimony, will-worship." (Colossians 2:1).

Eucharistia: "gratitude, grateful language (to God as an act of worship), thankfulness, giving of thanks." (Ephesians 5:4, Revelation 4:9).

Eucharisteo: "to be grateful, to express gratitude, to say grace at a meal." (Ephesians 5:20, Colossians 3:17, Revelation 11:17).

Euloged: "to speak well of, to bless, thank, invoke benediction on, bless, praise." (Matthew 21:9, Luke 1:64).

Eulogetos: "adorable, blessed." (Ephesians 1:3).

Eusebeo: "to be pious toward God, to worship, to respect, show piety, support (toward parents)." (Acts 17:23).

Hallomai: "to jump, to gush, leap, spring up." (Acts 3:8).

Homologeo: "to assent, covenant, acknowledge, confession is made, give thanks, promise." (Hebrews 13:15).

Hosanna: "oh save, an exclamation of adoration." (Matthew 21:9, Mark 11:10).

Kauchema: "a boast, to glory, glorifying, rejoice." (Hebrews 3:6).

Latreuo: "to minister, render religious homage, serve, to do service, worshipper." (Acts 24:11, Philippians 3:3, Hebrews 10:2).

Megaluno: "to make or declare great, increase or extol, enlarge, magnify, show great." (Luke 1:46, Acts 10:46).

Mousikos: "musical (as a noun), a minstrel, musician." (Revelation 18:22).

Proskunetes: "an adorer, a worshiper." (John 4:23-24).

Skirtao: "to jump, sympathetically move, leap for joy." (Luke 6:23).

Sebasma: "something adored, an object of worship (god, altar), devotion, that is worshiped." (2 Thessalonians 2:4).

Sebomai: "to revere, adore, devout, religious, worship." (Acts 18:7, Acts 16:14).

Sugchairo: "to sympathize in gladness, congratulate, rejoice." (Philippians 2:17).

Sumphonia: "unison of sound (symphony), a concert of instruments (harmonious note) music." (Luke 15:25).

Theosebes: "reverent towards God, a worshiper of God."(John 9:31).

Therapeuo: "to wait upon menially, to adore, to relieve of disease, cure, heal, worship." (Acts 17:25).

Threskeia: "ceremonial observance, religion, worshiping." (Colossians 2:18, Revelation 4:9).

Conclusion

Worship goes beyond our beautiful voices and presentation. Worship is a life full of love, holiness, and intimacy with God. There is a call for all ministers of music to seek a deeper life of consecration. We live in a season that pure worship is needed. It is time to step up to the next dimension in your call and challenge yourself, and avail yourself for a more significant move of God.

There is a cry for nations to bow in worship; will you be that vessel that our Father will find willing?

I pray your answer is Yes!

Bibliography

1. Dr. Rogers Barrier "Preach It, Teach It." "Are There Types of Praise in the Bible?" January 6, 2017, https://www.crosswalk.com/church/pastors-or-leadership/ask-roger/are-there-different-types-of-praise-in-the-bible.html

2. Gerrit Gusfason, Booklet-Be a Better Worshiper

3. Kairos Softwares LLC, Kairos Bible App for iphones, Strong's Concordance, Daily Verse Audio Dictionaries version 7.7

4. Just Worship, Resource for worshipers, Hebrew & Greek words for praise and worship www.justworship.com, http://justworship.com/greek-praise-words/, http://justworship.com/hebrew-words/

5. Bible dictionary & Glossary, by Webster, Easton and Smith, App developer Oleg Shukalovich

6. www.dictionary.com

Author's Bio

Pastor Elenora Mouphouet, known as "Pastor E" by her church congregation, preaches worship and biblical lessons through her first publication FREE2WORSHIP LIBERATED2PRAISE.

She was born in Liberia and currently resides in the United States of America. She and her husband, Apostle Edward Mouphouet, established Judah's Generation (JG), a para-church organization helping to restore the biblical principles of worship. She is the founder of Woman Arise Int'l, a network for pastor's wives, female clergy, and female church workers empowering them to be "a ready vessel...to leave a legacy."

Pastor Elenora inspires and preaches true worship globally through seminars, conferences, retreats, and her infamous "Atmosphere of Worship," preparing the stage for God and the miraculous. With over a decade of experience as a pastor and leader of worship, Pastor Elenora Mouphouet brings her passion to guide you back to Jesus' side through worship and prayer.

Contact
Email: pemministries1@gmail.com
Facebook Profile: Elenora Mouphouet (Pst E.)
Facebook Page: Pastor Elenora Mouphouet Ministries- PEMM
Instagram: @Pasemoup_ Official

www.ingramcontent.com/pod-product-compliance
Lightning Source LLC
Chambersburg PA
CBHW070133100426
42744CB00009B/1819